Marine Life For Young Readers

Seashells

Contents

Text by Stanley L. Swartz
Photography by Robert Yin

DOMINIE PRESS
Pearson Learning Group

About Seashells

Seashells are soft animals.

They live in hard shells.

Their shells **protect** their bodies.

◄ Seascape with Giant Clam Shell

There are more than 100,000 kinds of seashells. They are members of the **mollusk** family. Seashells live in the water.

◀ Tiger Cowry Shell

Seashells, Large and Small

Seashells come in many sizes.

Some seashells are **gigantic**.

Some are less than one inch long.

◄ Giant Clam with Underwater Photographer

How They See

Seashells have **tentacles**.

Each tentacle has one eye.

They can see in many directions.

◀ Strombus Shell

How They Move

Seashells have one foot. The foot is used to **crawl** or swim. Each kind of seashell has a different kind of foot.

◄ Volute Shell

Their Shapes and Colors

Seashells come in many shapes.
They also come in many colors.
Minerals in the water cause the
different colors.

◄ Tridacna Clam

Most seashells are very colorful.

The colors help **camouflage** them.

Seashells live in sand and under rocks.

◄ Simnia Shell

More About Seashells

Seashells breathe through **gills**.

They lay many eggs.

They eat small plants and animals.

◀ Lima Shell

A special sac holds the seashell's **organs**.

The sac is covered by the shell.

The shell is their home.

 Scallop

Seashell Products

Jewelry can be made from seashells. The shells are also used to make buttons.

◄ Map Cowry Shell

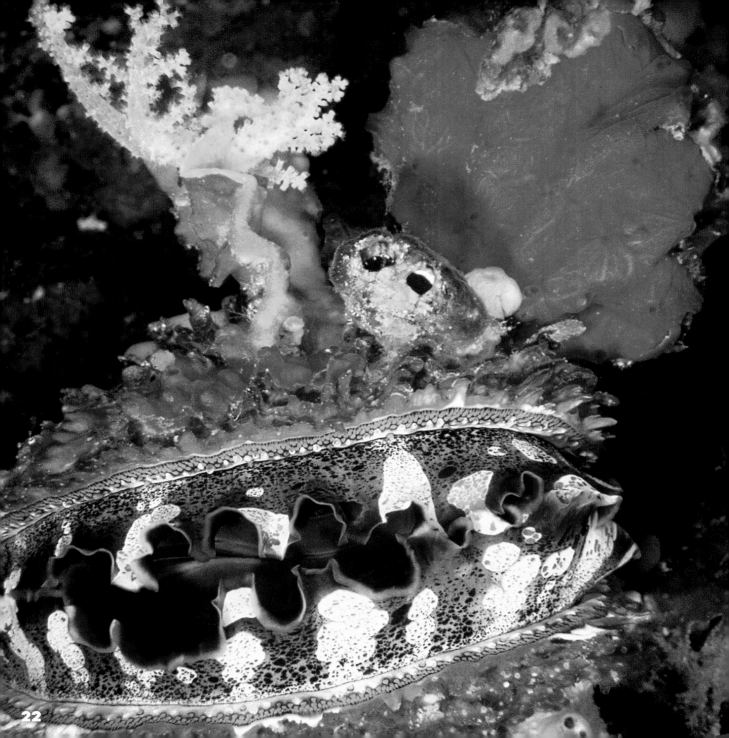

Seashell Collectables

Seashells leave their shells when they die. Some shells are found on the beach. People collect seashells as a **hobby**.

◀ Spiny Oyster Shell

Glossary

camouflage: To hide something, using a cover or disguise

crawl: To move slowly

gigantic: Very big

gills: A water creature's body part used for breathing

hobby: Collecting for fun

jewelry: Rings, necklaces, and earrings

minerals: Natural substances that are not living

mollusk: A sea animal with a soft body and a shell

organs: Important parts of the body, such as the heart or the brain

protect: To keep from harm

tentacles: Long body parts used to see or feel

Index